Get Set Go Phonics

Cinderella

Phonics Consultant Susan Purcell

Illustrator Giuliana Gregori

Concept Fran Bromage

Miles Kelly

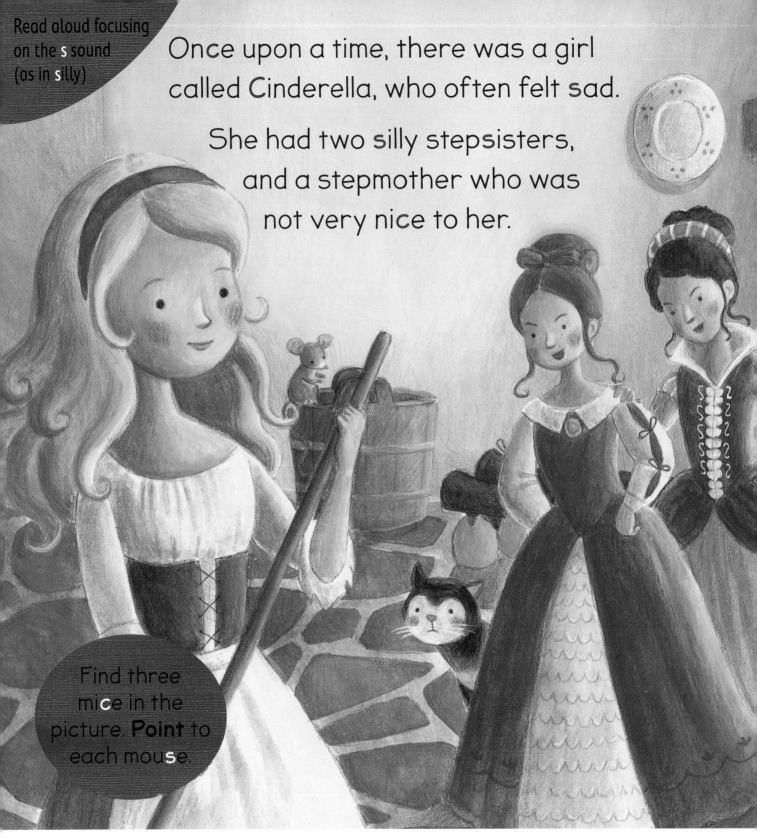

Once upon a time, there was a girl called Cinderella, who often felt **s**ad.

She had two **s**illy **s**tep**s**ister**s**, and a **s**tepmother who was not very ni**c**e to her.

Find three mi**c**e in the picture. **Point** to each mou**s**e.

Say the names as you spot each person in the picture.

Cinderella

sister

sister

Cinderella worked hard, but the sisters were never satisfied. Every night Cinderella sat by the fireside with the mice.

Sound out these words with the s sound.

ice   saucer   set   sell

circus   city   ceiling

One day the two stepsisters were being beastly to Cinderella, when a letter arrived.

It was an invitation to a ball at the palace, but Cinderella's stepmother banned her from going.

Spot the word that doesn't begin with the b sound.

bake   box   bear   bird   dog

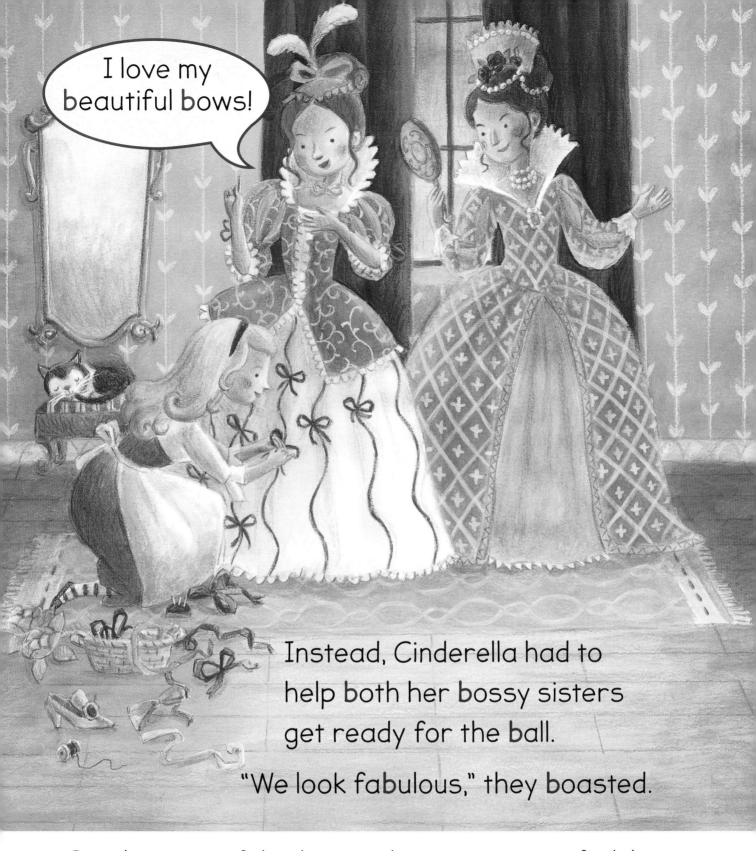

I love my beautiful bows!

Instead, Cinderella had to help both her bossy sisters get ready for the ball.

"We look fabulous," they boasted.

Say the names of the things in the pictures as you find them. They all use the b sound.

bows **beads** **ribbons**
bucket **basket**

I don't want to stay here.

As the carriage disappeared, Cinderella felt tears come to her eyes.

The palace was so near, but Cinderella feared she would never see inside it.

Sound out these words with the ear sound.

year   clear   beard

cheer   steer   deer

Suddenly, an old woman with glittery wings and a wand appeared!

"I'm your fairy godmother!" she said with a wave of her wand. "You will have your wish and go to the ball!"

Emphasize the w sound (as in wand)

"First, we will need to find some things," she said, with a wink.

Spot the word that doesn't begin with the w sound.

week   vest   wool   winter

"Bring me a pumpkin please," said Cinderella's fairy godmother.

With a twitch of a wing and a swing of her wand, she flung fairy magic high into the air!

Spot the word that doesn't end with the **ng** sound.

thing   young   very   along

A big, ripe pumpkin from the vegetable patch grew so big it looked as if it was ready to pop!

Sound out these words with the p sound in different positions.

park   poster   paper   puppy

chip   sheep   cheap

The enormous pumpkin transformed into a beautiful carriage, while four mice became stunning white horses!

Sound out these words with the or sound.

fork   corn   born   sport

short   pour   your

As the magic swirled around, a brown rat turned into a coachman and Cinderella clapped her hands.

Spot the word that doesn't use the a sound.

map flag ant gown apple

Sound out the blends cl and gl as you read

With a clap of her hands, Cinderella's clever fairy godmother turned Cinderella's plain clothes into a glamorous gown.

Cinderella's hair became glossy, and on her feet were glittery glass slippers.

Sound out these words beginning with the cl and gl blends.

cloud   click   class   club

glove   glad   glue

Cinderella glowed with happiness.

"Keep a close eye on the clock," warned the fairy godmother. "The spell will end when the clock strikes twelve."

Spot the word that doesn't begin with the cl or gl blend.

climb   doll   glow   glare

Emphasize the air sound (as in hair)

As Cinderella arrived at the palace, wearing her stunning gown and with jewels in her hair, everyone turned to stare. "Who is that fair lady?" asked the prince.

Cinderella's stepsisters didn't recognize her, but they glared as she walked down the stairs.

Spot the word that doesn't end with the air sound.

there   chair   more   share

The prince spun Cinderella into the middle of the room.

They danced all night by the light of the moon.

The prince felt he had found his true love.

Sound out these words with the oo sound.

spoon   zoo   blue   glue

chew   threw

15

highlight
ie sound
(as in tie)

While the dancing carried on into the night, the clock struck twelve.

Cinderella gave a frightened cry – she hadn't noticed the time!"

As she ran down the flight of steps she left behind a glass slipper.

Sound out some words with the ie sound.

mine   smile   wild   find

tie   pie   try   by   might

Cinderella jumped into the carriage, but the magic wore off just as she started the journey home.

The carriage turned back into a giant pumpkin, the horses became mice and her gown and jewels vanished.

As you read, foc
on the j sou
(as in just)

Spot the word that doesn't begin with the j sound.

jug   jelly   yellow   giraffe

The handsome prince's heart was heavy. He had fallen in love with Cinderella, and wanted to visit every house in his country with her glass slipper.

Say the words as you spot things beginning with the h sound.

hand

hat

hair

"I will hunt high and low," said the prince. "Whoever this slipper fits shall be my bride."

Soon he arrived at Cinderella's home.

Sound out these words with the h sound.

hill   help   hold   hurry

whose   whole

The prince called everyone in to try on the slipper. Of course, the stepsisters' feet couldn't fit.

Cinderella stood quietly in the corner. "Can you try it too?" asked the prince.

Say the words as you spot things beginning with the k sound.

cushion

cat

candle

"She can't try it on; she works in the kitchen," replied Cinderella's cunning stepmother.

The kind prince lifted Cinderella's foot onto the cushion. The slipper fitted! No one could believe it.

Emphasize the k sound as you say this sentence together.

"She can't try it on;
she works in the kitchen."

"I've found you!" said the kind prince. He took Cinderella's hand in his, and asked her to marry him.

Her stepsisters could only stand by and watch as the prince and Cinderella became husband and wife.

Spot the word that doesn't end with the nd blend.

send   band   girl   pond

Ask your child to **retell** the story using
these key sounds and story images.

Cinderella

bossy

wish

horses

stare

room

cry

hunt

husband

set   city   saucer   ice   silly

cheer   beard   deer   year

bring   young   along   swing

pumpkin   chip   pop   patch

map   hand   rat   flag   magic

cloud   click   clock   clap

glad   glove   glossy   glow

jug   giant   giraffe   jelly

cat   kitchen   candle   kind

You've had fun with phonics! Well done.

24